Dinosaurs Dominate

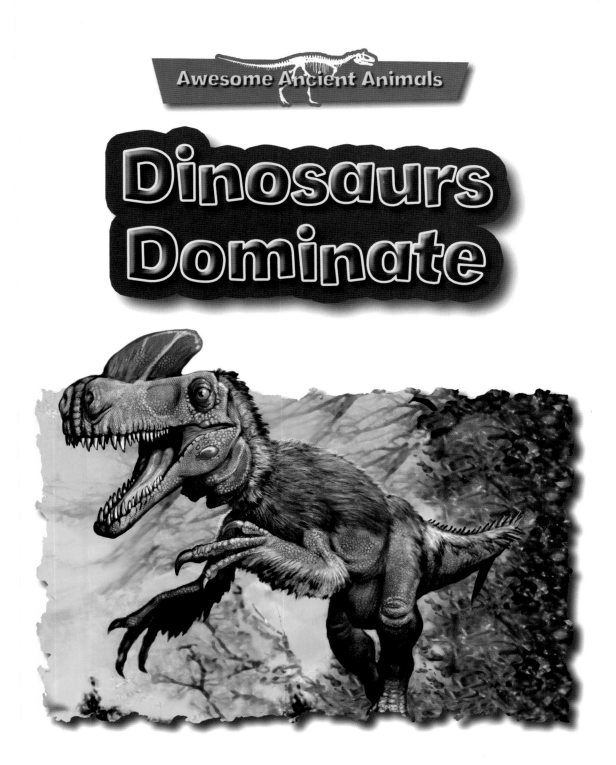

Jurassic Life

Dougal Dixon

An Hachette Company

First published in the United States by
New Forest Press, an imprint of Octopus Publishing Group Ltd

www.octopusbook.usa.com

Copyright © Octopus Publishing Group Ltd 2012

Published by arrangement with Black Rabbit Books

PO Box 784, Mankato, MN 56002

Library of Congress Cataloging-in-Publication Data

Dixon, Dougal.
Dinosaurs Dominate : Jurassic Life / by Dougal Dixon.
p. cm. -- (Awesome Ancient Animals)
Summary: "Describes some of the animals of the Jurassic Period, a
time when dinosaurs reached their biggest sizes. Includes an Animal
Families glossary, prehistory timeline, and pronunciation guides"--
Provided by publisher.
Includes index.
ISBN 978-1-84898-628-2 (hardcover, library bound)
1. Paleontology--Jurassic--Juvenile literature. 2. Dinosaurs--
Juvenile literature. I. Title.
QE733.D588 2013
560'.1766--dc23
2012002749

Printed and bound in the USA

16 15 14 13 12 1 2 3 4 5

Publisher: Tim Cook Editor: Margaret Parrish Designer: Steve West

Contents

Introduction

This map shows how the Earth looked in the Jurassic Period. The Earth was mostly desert. By the end of the Jurassic, the continents were dividing.

This map shows how the Earth looks today. See how different it is! The continents have split up and moved around.

Awesome Ancient Animals follows the evolution of animals.

The Earth's history is divided into eras, which are divided into periods. These last millions of years. *Dinosaurs Dominate* takes you back to the Jurassic Period, when dinosaurs reached their hugest sizes. Some were bigger than whales, others as small as foxes.

A LOOK BACK IN TIME

This timeline shows how simple creatures evolved into many differnt and complex life-forms. This took millions and millions of years. In the chart, MYA stands for million years ago.

	BOOK	PERIOD	
CENOZOIC ERA	THE ICE AGE	1.81 MYA to now QUATERNARY	This is a time of Ice Ages and mammals. Our direct relatives, Homo sapiens, appear.
	ANCIENT MAMMALS	65 to 1.81 MYA TERTIARY	Giant mammals and huge, hunting birds rule. Our first human relatives start to evolve.
MESOZOIC ERA	CRETACEOUS LIFE	145 to 65 MYA CRETACEOUS	Huge dinosaurs evolve. They die out by the end of this period.
	JURASSIC LIFE	200 to 145 MYA JURASSIC	Large and small dinosaurs and flying creatures develop.
	TRIASSIC LIFE	250 to 200 MYA TRIASSIC	The "Age of Dinosaurs" begins. Early mammals live alongside them.
PALEOZOIC ERA	EARLY LIFE	299 to 250 MYA PERMIAN	Sail-backed reptiles start to appear.
		359 to 299 MYA CARBONIFEROUS	The first reptiles appear and tropical forests develop.
		416 to 359 MYA DEVONIAN	Bony fish evolve. Trees and insects come on the scene.
		444 to 416 MYA SILURIAN	Fish with jaws develop and sea animals start living on land.
		488 to 444 MYA ORDOVICIAN	Primitive fish, trilobites, shellfish, and plants evolve.
		542 to 488 MYA CAMBRIAN	First animals with skeletons appear.

Ichthyosaurus

In the Mesozoic Era, the ocean teemed with swimming reptiles. The ichthyosaurs, or "fish-lizards," were some of the most common. When they first appeared, ichthyosaurs were huge whalelike animals. By the Jurassic Period, the ichthyosaurs, including *Ichthyosaurus*, were smaller and more like dolphins.

Ichthyosaurs gave birth to live young. They did not lay eggs. Fossils of baby ichthyosaurs being born have been found.

Ichthyosaurus was a speedy hunter. It chased and caught the fastest fish and squidlike animals of the time.

Animal fact file

NAME: ICHTHYOSAURUS (FISH LIZARD)

PRONOUNCED: IK-THEE-OH-SORE-USS

GROUP: ICHTHYOSAURS

WHERE IT LIVED: WORLDWIDE

WHEN IT LIVED: EARLY JURASSIC PERIOD (200 TO 176 MILLION YEARS AGO)

LENGTH: 7 FT (2.1 M)

SPECIAL FEATURES: MOST STREAMLINED AND FISHLIKE OF THE REPTILES

FOOD: FISH AND CEPHALOPODS

MAIN ENEMY: PLIOSAURS

DID YOU KNOW?: USUALLY THE SOFT, FLESHY PARTS OF ANIMALS DO NOT FOSSILIZE, BUT SOME ICHTHYOSAURUS FOSSILS INCLUDE PRESERVED FINS.

Cryptoclidus

The plesiosaurs were some of the most important swimming reptiles of the Jurassic Period. There were two types—those with long necks and those with short necks. *Cryptoclidus* was a long-necked plesiosaur.

"Like a snake threaded through a turtle" was how one early paleontologiest described the plesiosaur. The long neck, broad body, and paddles give this impression.

Cryptoclidus flew through the water. Its front paddles worked like wings, while the hind paddles acted as stabilizers.

Animal fact file

NAME: CRYPTOCLIDUS (HIDDEN COLLAR BONE)

PRONOUNCED: CRIP-TOE-CLIDE-US

GROUP: LONG-NECKED PLESIOSAURS

WHERE IT LIVED: EUROPE

WHEN IT LIVED: LATE JURASSIC PERIOD (161 TO 145 MILLION YEARS AGO)

LENGTH: 26 FT (8 M)

SPECIAL FEATURES: LONG POINTED TEETH, IDEAL FOR CATCHING SLIPPERY PREY

FOOD: FISH AND SQUID

MAIN ENEMY: SHORT-NECKED PLESIOSAURS, SUCH AS LIOPLEURODON

DID YOU KNOW?: FOSSILS FORM MORE EASILY IN THE SEA THAN ON LAND, SO FOSSILS FROM SWIMMING REPTILES ARE FAIRLY COMMON. SCIENTISTS WERE STUDYING PLESIOSAUR FOSSILS LONG BEFORE THEY DISCOVERED DINOSAUR FOSSILS.

Liopleurodon

The biggest reptiles of the Jurassic seas, and probably the biggest meat-eating animals of all time, were the short-necked plesiosaurs. They had very long jaws, like a crocodile's. The biggest of them was the huge *Liopleurodon*.

Liopleurodon probably swallowed stones to make it sink in the water; to surface, it spit them out. Its streamlined body made it very quick and its massive jaws gave it a bite stronger than *Tyrannosaurus*.

This is the tooth of a *Liopleurodon*. It is about 8 in (20 cm) long. Bite marks found on the bones of ichthyosaurs and other plesiosaurs, show that *Liopleurodon* was a fierce predator.

Animal fact file

NAME: LIOPLEURODON (SMOOTH-SIDED TOOTH)

PRONOUNCED: LIE-OH-PLOOR-OH-DON

GROUP: SHORT-NECKED PLESIOSAURS

WHERE IT LIVED: NORTHERN EUROPE

WHEN IT LIVED: LATE JURASSIC PERIOD (161 TO 145 MILLION YEARS AGO)

LENGTH: 49 FT (15 M)

SPECIAL FEATURES: THE BIGGEST SEA REPTILE OF THE TIME

FOOD: OTHER SEA REPTILES

MAIN ENEMY: NONE

DID YOU KNOW?: SHORT-NECKED PLESIOSAURS COULD BE AS SMALL AS A PENGUIN OR AS LARGE AS A SPERM WHALE.

Pterodactylus

The skies were full of flying animals in the Late Jurassic Period, including insects and the first birds. The most important flying animals were reptiles, the pterosaurs. There were two groups of pterosaur: the long-tailed pterosaurs and the short-tailed pterosaurs. *Pterodactylus* was a short-tailed pterosaur.

Well-preserved pterosaur fossils are common. Here, the spine and neck bones can be clearly seen. In some fossils, even the wing membrane is visible.

Each species of *Pterodactylus* was adapted to eat a particular food. Smaller ones were probably insect-eaters; larger one likely ate fish or small lizards.

Animal fact file

NAME: PTERODACTYLUS (WING FINGER)

PRONOUNCED: TEH-ROE-DACK-TILL-US

GROUP: PTERODACTYLOIDS— THE SHORT-TAILED PTEROSAURS

WHERE IT LIVED: NORTHERN EUROPE AND AFRICA

WHEN IT LIVED: LATE JURASSIC PERIOD (161 TO 145 MILLION YEARS AGO)

WINGSPAN: 3 FT (1 M)

SPECIAL FEATURES: BROAD WINGS, A SHORT TAIL AND A LONG NECK

FOOD: FISH AND SMALL REPTILES

MAIN ENEMY: LARGER PTEROSAURS

DID YOU KNOW?: SCIENTISTS FIRST THOUGHT THAT PTEROSAURS WERE SWIMMING ANIMALS AND THAT ITS WINGS WERE FINS.

Camptosaurus

Camptosaurus was a two-footed, plant-eating dinosaur. It spent much of its time on its hind legs, reaching high into trees in search of food. The bigger individuals were too heavy to spend too much time on their hind legs and must have walked on all fours.

Camptosaurus lived in thick, riverside forests. It probably ran in herds, as many plant-eating animals do today. Herds offered protection from meat-eaters.

Camptosaurus and its relatives had cheeks like we do. This allowed them to chew their food before swallowing it and made digesting food easier. Plant-eating dinosaurs with long necks swallowed their food whole.

Animal fact file

NAME: CAMPTOSAURUS (FLEXIBLE LIZARD)

PRONOUNCED: CAMP-TOE-SORE-US

GROUP: ORNITHOPOD DINOSAURS

WHERE IT LIVED: WESTERN PARTS OF THE UNITED STATES

WHEN IT LIVED: LATE JURASSIC PERIOD (161 TO 145 MILLION YEARS AGO)

LENGTH: 23 FT (7 M)

SPECIAL FEATURES: SMALL HEAD, STRONG BEAK, GRINDING TEETH

FOOD: LOW-GROWING PLANTS

MAIN ENEMY: BIG MEAT-EATING DINOSAURS LIKE ALLOSAURUS

DID YOU KNOW?: SKELETONS OF CAMPTOSAURUS WERE FOUND IN THE 1880S.

Heterodontosaurus

Heterodontosaurus looks like a fierce meat-eater. But this was just an aggressive pose. It was actually a plant-eating dinosaur that probably scared away its enemies by pretending to be fearsome. If that did not work, it was small and light enough to run away quickly.

Heterodontosaurus has one of the best-preserved dinosaur skeletons known. The fossils were found in South Africa in 1966. It had long hind legs for running and short arms with little hands for grasping.

This skull fossil shows a long side tusk. It is likely that only males had these. They were probably used during mating to scare away rivals. Like other ornithopods, *Heterodontosaurus* had a birdlike beak.

Animal fact file

NAME: HETERODONTOSAURUS (LIZARD WITH DIFFERENTLY SHAPED TEETH)

PRONOUNCED: HET-ER-OH-DON-TOE-SORE-US

GROUP: ORNITHOPOD DINOSAURS

WHERE IT LIVED: SOUTH AFRICA

WHEN IT LIVED: EARLY JURASSIC PERIOD (200 TO 190 MILLION YEARS AGO)

LENGTH: 4 FT (1.2 M)

SPECIAL FEATURES: THREE KINDS OF TEETH—NIPPING TEETH IN THE BEAK, TUSKS ON THE SIDE, GRINDING TEETH AT THE BACK

FOOD: PLANTS

MAIN ENEMY: MEAT-EATING DINOSAURS AND CROCODILES

DID YOU KNOW?: HETERODONTOSAURUS HAD FIVE FINGERS, BUT TWO WERE TINY.

Scutellosaurus

One of the earliest armored dinosaurs was *Scutellosaurus*. Its neck, back, and long tail were covered in tiny armored, bonelike shields and its legs were long and thin. In later periods, armored dinosaurs grew very big, but *Scutellosaurus* was the size of a small dog.

Scutellosaurus could run on its hind legs, although its armor would have been heavy. It probably spent most of its time on all fours.

Scutellosaurus had a small head in comparison to the size of its body. As a plant-eating dinosaur, its jaw was only strong enough to munch on leaves.

Animal fact file

NAME: SCUTELLOSAURUS (LIZARD WITH LITTLE SHIELDS)

PRONOUNCED: SCOO-TEL-OH-SORE-US

GROUP: THYREOPHORAN DINOSAURS

WHERE IT LIVED: UNITED STATES

WHEN IT LIVED: EARLY JURASSIC PERIOD (200 TO 190 MILLION YEARS AGO)

LENGTH: 4 FT (1.2 M), MOST OF WHICH WAS ITS TAIL

SPECIAL FEATURES: COVERED IN SEVERAL KINDS OF ARMOR, INCLUDING OVAL PLATES ALONG THE SIDE AND A RIDGE OF VERTICAL PLATES DOWN THE BACK AND TAIL.

FOOD: LOW-GROWING PLANTS

MAIN ENEMY: BIG MEAT-EATING DINOSAURS

DID YOU KNOW?: ARMOR WAS SCUTELLOSAURUS'S MAIN DEFENSE. MEAT-EATING DINOSAURS WOULD HAVE HAD TROUBLE CHEWING THROUGH IT. SCUTELLOSAURUS ALSO RAN FROM DANGER.

Stegosaurus

One of the most recognizable of the armored dinosaurs was *Stegosaurus*. It had a double row of plates down the back. These were either covered in horn and used for defense, or covered in skin and used to keep the dinosaur warm—no one is certain which.

When the weather was cold *Stegosaurus* would have stood sideways to the sun, so sunlight could warm its plates. In the heat, *Stegosaurus* cooled off by facing its plates into the wind.

Stegosaurus had strong hips and hind legs, showing that it could rear up on two legs to eat from tree branches.

Animal fact file

NAME: STEGOSAURUS (ROOFED LIZARD)

PRONOUNCED: STEG-OH-SORE-US

GROUP: THYREOPHORAN DINOSAURS

WHERE IT LIVED: MIDWESTERN UNITED STATES

WHEN IT LIVED: LATE JURASSIC PERIOD (156 TO 145 MILLION YEARS AGO)

LENGTH: 30 FT (9 M)

SPECIAL FEATURES: TWO PAIRS OF SPIKES ON TAIL FOR DEFENSE

FOOD: PLANTS

MAIN ENEMY: BIG MEAT-EATING DINOSAURS LIKE ALLOSAURUS

DID YOU KNOW?: STEGOSAURUS'S BRAIN WAS SO SMALL THAT SCIENTISTS FIRST THOUGHT IT MUST HAVE HAD A SECOND BRAIN IN ITS HIPS TO CONTROL THE LEGS AND TAIL.

Brachiosaurus

Brachiosaurus was a long-necked plant-eating sauropod. There were many types of big sauropod in the Late Jurassic Period. Some were adapted for grazing on plants that grew close to the ground. Others, like *Brachiosaurus*, were tall so they could eat leaves and needles from high in the trees.

Brachiosaurus is one of the biggest land-dwelling animals known. However, its bones weren't that heavy. They were hollow, so they could be both long and lightweight.

Brachiosaurus was over 40 ft (12 m) tall, about the height of a four-story building.

Animal fact file

NAME: BRACHIOSAURUS (ARM LIZARD)

PRONOUNCED: BRACKEE-OH-SORE-US

GROUP: SAUROPOD DINOSAURS

WHERE IT LIVED: EAST AFRICA AND MIDWESTERN UNITED STATES

WHEN IT LIVED: MID TO LATE JURASSIC PERIOD (156 TO 145 MILLION YEARS AGO)

LENGTH: 79 FT (24 M)

SPECIAL FEATURES: LONG NECK, SMALL HEAD. THE TAIL WAS 25 FT (7.5 M) LONG— RELATIVELY SHORT FOR A SAUROPOD.

FOOD: LEAVES FROM TREES

MAIN ENEMY: BIG MEAT-EATING DINOSAURS LIKE ALLOSAURUS

DID YOU KNOW?: BRACHIOSAURUS FOSSILS HAVE BEEN FOUND IN BOTH AFRICA AND NORTH AMERICA, SHOWING THAT THE TWO CONTINENTS WERE CLOSE TOGETHER IN LATE JURASSIC TIMES.

Brachytrachelopan

Brachytrachelopan had the shortest neck of all sauropods. It had the same number of vertebrae as most sauropods, but they were more compact, making their necks much shorter than the others. *Brachytrachelopan* must have looked a lot like a *Stegosaurus*, but without armor plates.

Most sauropods had long necks. However, *Brachytrachelopan* fossils show it had a short neck. It must have eaten plants growing on the ground right in front of it.

Brachytrachelopan had a high ridge down its back. This may have held the strong muscles needed to support its neck. Or it may have been brightly colored and used to signal to other dinosaurs—either to attract a mate or to warn rivals away.

Animal fact file

NAME: BRACHYTRACHELOPAN (SHORT-NECKED SHEPHERD GOD)

PRONOUNCED: BRACK-EE-TRACK-ELL-OH-PAN

GROUP: SAUROPOD DINOSAURS

WHERE IT LIVED: ARGENTINA

WHEN IT LIVED: LATE JURASSIC PERIOD (150 MILLION YEARS AGO)

LENGTH: 25 FT (7.5 M)

SPECIAL FEATURES: SHORT NECK

FOOD: LOW-GROWING PLANTS

MAIN ENEMY: BIG MEAT-EATING DINOSAURS

DID YOU KNOW?: ONLY HALF OF ONE SKELETON HAS BEEN FOUND; ALL WE KNOW ABOUT THIS CREATURE COMES FROM THAT.

Allosaurus

The biggest and fiercest of the meat-eating dinosaurs in the Late Jurassic Period was *Allosaurus*. It was big enough to hunt the largest of the plant-eating sauropods, although, like lions and tigers today, it probably concentrated on the young, the old, and the injured.

With the big claws on its three-fingered hands, *Allosaurus* seized its prey. It then killed its victim with knifelike teeth. Small scavenging dinosaurs and pterosaurs ate what *Allosaurus* left behind.

Over 40 skeletons of *Allosaurus* were found in a single quarry in Utah. Most *Allosaurus* skeletons in museums today come from this site.

Animal fact file

NAME: ALLOSAURUS (DIFFERENT LIZARD)

PRONOUNCED: AL-OH-SORE-US

GROUP: THEROPOD DINOSAURS

WHERE IT LIVED: WESTERN UNITED STATES

WHEN IT LIVED: LATE JURASSIC PERIOD (156 TO 145 MILLION YEARS AGO)

LENGTH: 38 FT (11.5 M)

SPECIAL FEATURES: THE BIGGEST LAND-DWELLING MEAT-EATER OF THE TIME

FOOD: BIG PLANT-EATING DINOSAURS, LIKE STEGOSAURUS OR BRACHIOSAURUS

MAIN ENEMY: NONE

DID YOU KNOW?: ALLOSAURUS WEIGHED AROUND 5.5 TONS (5 METRIC TONS)—ABOUT THE WEIGHT OF AN ELEPHANT. THERE WERE SEVERAL SMALLER SPECIES, SOME WEIGHING ONLY 1 TON—WHICH IS STILL HEAVY.

Guanlong

The most famous meat-eating dinosaur ever must be *Tyrannosaurus rex. Guanlong* was one of its earliest relatives, although it was small in comparison. It was just as fierce, however, even though it hunted smaller prey.

Most active animals are warm-blooded. Hair or feathers help them control their body temperature. Scientists think the small, meat-eating dinosaurs were warm-blooded and probably had feathery coverings.

Animal fact file

NAME: GUANLONG (CROWNED DRAGON)

PRONOUNCED: GWON-LONG

GROUP: THEROPOD DINOSAURS

WHERE IT LIVED: CHINA

WHEN IT LIVED: LATE JURASSIC PERIOD (160 MILLION YEARS AGO)

LENGTH: 10 FT (3 M)

SPECIAL FEATURES: THE EARLIEST TYRANNOSAUR KNOWN

FOOD: OTHER DINOSAURS

MAIN ENEMY: BIGGER MEAT-EATING DINOSAURS

DID YOU KNOW?: UNTIL GUANLONG WAS DISCOVERED, SCIENTISTS THOUGHT THAT TYRANNOSAURS LIVED ONLY IN CRETACEOUS TIMES.

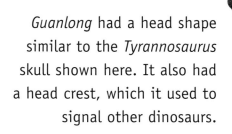

Guanlong had a head shape similar to the *Tyrannosaurus* skull shown here. It also had a head crest, which it used to signal other dinosaurs.

Animal Families Glossary

Cephalopods—literally the "head-footed" animals. The modern types, the octopus and squid, seem to have legs branching from their faces. In prehistoric times many cephalopods had chambered shells.

Ichthyosaurs—a group of seagoing reptiles. They were well-adapted to life in the sea and looked like dolphins or sharks. They had fins on their tails and backs, and paddles for limbs. Ichthyosaurs were common in the Triassic and the Jurassic periods but died out in the Cretaceous.

Ornithopods—the plant-eating dinosaurs group that usually walked two legs. They were present throughout the late Triassic and Jurassic periods but it was in the later Cretaceous that they became really important.

Plesiosaurs—the group of swimming reptiles with paddle-shaped limbs and flat bodies. There were two types—the long-necked forms and the whalelike short-necked forms. They lived throughout dinosaur times.

Pterodactyloids—one of the two groups of pterosaurs. These had short tails and long necks, unlike the other group, the rhamphorhynchoids, which had long tails and short necks.

Pterosaurs—the flying reptiles of the age of dinosaurs. They had broad leathery wings supported on a long fourth finger and were covered in hair to keep them warm.

Sauropods—the plant-eating dinosaur group that had huge bodies, long necks, and long tails. They were the biggest land-dwelling animals that ever lived, and reached their peak in late Jurassic times.

Theropod—the meat-eating dinosaur group. They all had the same shape—long jaws with sharp teeth, long strong hind legs, smaller front legs with clawed hands, and a small body balanced by a long tail.

Thyreophorans—the armored dinosaur group. There were two main lines. The first to develop were the plated stegosaurs, and later came the armor-covered ankylosaurs.

Tyrannosaurs—one of the theropod dinosaur groups. At the end of the Cretaceous Period they were among the biggest meat-eaters of all time, but the early forms, in the late Jurassic, were small animals.

Glossary

Adapted—changing to survive in a particular habitat or weather conditions.

Cephalopod—an animal that lives in the ocean and has a big head and tentacles, such as an octopus.

Continent—one of the world's main landmasses, such as Africa and Europe.

Evolution—changes or developments that happen to all forms of life over millions of years as a result of changes in the environment.

Evolve—to change or develop.

Fossil—the remains of a prehistoric plant or animal that has been buried for a long time and become hardened in rock.

Grinding teeth—these are teeth used to chew food.

Hollow bones—bones that have a space inside them so that they are not solid. Hollow bones are much lighter than solid bones.

Nipping teeth—these are teeth used to bite leaves off the trees.

Ornithopod—a type of plant-eating dinosaur.

Paleontologist—a scientist who studies fossils.

Plesiosaur—a reptile that lived in the sea.

Prey—animals that are hunted by other animals as food.

Quarry—a place where stones are dug up for building.

Sauropod—a large plant-eating dinosaur.

Spine—the backbone of an animal.

Stabilizer—something, such as a tail, that helps an animal keep its balance.

Streamlined—an animal with a smooth, bullet-shaped body that allows it move through air or water easily and quickly.

Trilobite—an early type of sea animal that no longer exists.

Tyrannosaur—a type of large meat-eating dinosaur.

Vertebrae—small bones that form the backbone.

Vertical plate—a flat bone that stood upright on the backs of some dinosaurs.

Warm-blooded—animals, such as small mammals, that always have the same body temperature.

Well-preserved—a fossil that is in good condition.

Wing membrane—a thin sheet of skin attached to bone that forms a wing.

Index

Picture credits

Main image: 20-21, 26-27 Simon Mendez; 10-11 Bob Nicholls; 6-7, 8-9, 12-13, 14-15, 16-17, 18-19, 22-23, 24-25, 28-29 Luis Rey 4TL, 4TR, 5 (Cenozoic Era) 7, 9, 11, 12, 15, 20, 25, 26 Ticktock Media archive; 5 (Mesozoic Era top, Paleozoic Era top) Simon Mendez; 5 (Mesozoic Era center, Paleozoic Era bottom) Luis Rey; 5 (Mesozoic Era bottom) Lisa Alderson; 16 The Natural History Museum, London; 19 Chris Tomlin; 23 Louie Psihoyos/Corbis; 29 Tyler Olson/Shutterstock

Every effort has been made to trace the copyright holders and we apologize in advance for any unintentional omissions. We would be pleased to insert the appropriate acknowledgment in any subsequent edition of this publication.